that person himself

Other works by Gerry Loose include:

Change (images by K. Sweeney McGee)
Yuga Night (with Larry Butler & Kathleen McGee)
Knockariddera
a measure
Eitgal
Being Time
The Elementary Particles
Tongues of Stone
Printed on Water — New & Selected Poems
the deer path to my door

as editor

The Holistic Handbook
Seed Catalogue (with Morven Gregor)
Ten Seasons: explorations in botanics
                (with photographs by Morven Gregor)

as editor & translator

The Botanical Basho (with Yushin Toda)

Gerry Loose

that person himself

Shearsman Books
Exeter

First published in in the United Kingdom in 2009 by
Shearsman Books Ltd
58 Velwell Road
Exeter EX4 4LD

www.shearsman.com

ISBN 978-1-84861-038-5
First Edition
Copyright © Gerry Loose, 2009.

The right of Gerry Loose to be identified as the author of this work
has been asserted by him in accordance with the
Copyrights, Designs and Patents Act of 1988.
All rights reserved.

Acknowledgements

Some of this work appeared at http://www.archiveofthenow.com. An earlier version of the opening passages appeared on DVD as part of Camcorder Guerillas' *Voices for Vanunu*. Extracts appeared on the walls of the Cooper Gallery, Barnsley, January–February 2007 as part of the *Talking Points Local Marks Global Impressions* exhibition.

Thanks are due to Tom Leonard, Peter Manson, Larry Butler & Graham Hartill, who read drafts & who all made valuable suggestions.
Thanks particularly to Morven Gregor who read the manuscript as it was being written & offered encouragement & insight.
Thanks also to Iain Orr.

that person himself was completed in draft at Hotel Chevillon, Grez sur Loing, where I spent two months in 2006, made possible by a Robert Louis Stevenson Fellowship; I am grateful for this opportunity to the Scottish Arts Council & the National Library of Scotland.

Field research was made possible by a grant from the Scottish Arts Council.

In addition, I am grateful to Jim Mac Ritchie & Andrew Schelling in Boulder & to Masayuki Ebinuma in Nagasaki who all gave me room in their houses when it was needed. Andrew Schelling also shed much light for me on passages of the *Bhagavad Gita*.

The book would not have happened without the testimony of the many survivors quoted in these pages – verbatim. To them, their memory & to all those to whom I spoke, I extend my humblest & deepest gratitude.

for hibakusha

early morning
squints
clears his throat

thin pickings among a low
use segment of the population
desert
a damn good place to dump
used razor blades

himself
barkingdog

threadbare changing tricky
liar steal your teethfillings
in a gasmask

inventing climate
barkingdog the mushroom
oregon honey mushroom biggest cloud
all the states
swelling bursting cloud oh
barkingdog howlinwolf
wind

inventing a merika
barkingdog driving
SUV big as a hog
face of anubis
gaspetrol fuelrod litres
countless // desert sands & so on
little saudis in tank
that person toadpoop fart shit

all the states

sez all the names of all
the states laughs out loud all
the names ha ha runs downwind on 2
legs
roadrunner heh heh
andale andale whee where

                                        State of Nevada
Jack's voice box, they scraped what they could get, his tongue swelled so that it burst out of his mouth and covered his nose

Daddy's flesh was deteriorating, his flesh was cracking open, his flesh came off the bone, his hip bones came through the flesh, his stomach busted loose, his penis was larger than a horse swollen up with all that corruption; blood would come out of his eyes

Hap has no stomach muscles, his bladder is backwards, his teeth laying sideways

barkingfox

the space in the ear
where once noise was

himself as dust what d'you call
those dust things sizzle & whirl

on the spot up into sky dervish
spiralling doric cyclone
syzygy twister

Do any of the following apply to you?
(Answer Yes or No)
Do you have a communicable disease?

Physical or mental disorder?

in the beginning is lost
interesting to have headline
headstone at story's end
going & going

that person
steals a lot
stuff to hand
dishes
pitchers
a bear or two
anathemas
himself
sneezes *ash ayish totsooooh*
into darkness up
wards & little stars
appear
disordered stuck
snot

New Mexico:
Kirtland Air Force Base
A judge dismissed misdemeanor charges against Andrew McDaniel, a former Kirtland Air Force Base sergeant, accused of burning a 5-foot wooden cross in his yard. The state failed to provide a list of witnesses, the judge ruled.

going & going. going & going.
wandering hot among
cactus hot among joshua trees
wonders who joshua before joshua
going & going. too hot to
wander lays head to rest
stone for pillow head to rest

wakes refreshed early morning
cool going & going. left
on the pillowstone his head
so forgetful going & wandering

head on pillowstone
dreamingstone storystone a star

venus whispers what a fine
what a flash what a fine fire

He who dwells in the body can never be slain therefore you do not need to grieve for any living being

State of California
Robert's six feet of intestines removed, colostomy; eviscerated at 30 years of age

every stone here a star
the old fellers picked
names Badger
Bear
Lightning Rattle
Parrot
Roadrunner
Speech
Displaying Woman
Quetzal
Venus
Waving Person
those who came first
stories to newcomers
seen it all

fine fire right there
in the middle
Socorro
Sierra Oscura
Jornada del Muerto
what a trinity

oh must be he's sleeping

holy smoke popped
ten thousand stinkbugs
right there whoosh
beef cooked on a thousand
steers right there whoosh oy ha
saw what they'd done
shit emselves

State of California
Rulon had a cow that had a calf once born without a tail during that time, just no sign of that tail at all. One cow had a three legged calf

Are you a drug abuser or addict?

SPEED MONITORED BY AIRCRAFT

Although no information on the test was released until after the atomic bomb was used as a weapon against Japan, people in New Mexico knew something had happened. The shock wave broke windows 120 miles away and was felt by many at least 160 miles away. Army officials simply stated that a munitions storage area had accidently (sic) exploded at the Alamogordo Bombing Range.
The explosion did not make much of a crater. Most eyewitnesses describe the area as more of a small depression

ATOM BOMB TRINITITE

OPEN

Support Our Troops

Coca Cola

Have you ever been or are you now involved in espionage?
Or sabotage? Or in terrorist activities? Or genocide?

never said it'd be easy
stinkbug to barkinfox
sitting on a buffalo
sorry bluff
nope
but we're winning

one a them cockatrices
trappists theorists *no*
terroirists
too small for a beard
tried to pull auntie's
legs off

what are they like
squirted him good hnh
now he smells a shit smells a puke
like sleeping in a cesspit
bad cess bad
cess

trappists did I say
jews meant the other ones muslims
always getting em confused
them & mormons
people of the boke

        Considering your specific duty you
        should know there is no better

                              engagement than fighting on religious
                              principles and so no need for hesitation
stinkbug beginning to annoy

going & hmm
saucy rump two twisters coming
out of her head brains
or horns wonders him
self licking
lips speaking out
of both sides of his mouth
hey fine horns you got I've
got a horn too what's your name how about swapping horns mine's
powerful spits bettern stinkbug they all love it
hornbrain just
looks big eyes chewing
chewing saying nothing
himself keeping on
's a fine longhorn it sings like Lark moves like Sidewinder gobbles like
Loon here try it I'll
just screw it on from behind diggety call it call it Hound Dog
& she chewing
gazing dreamyeyed
o she says O sez
mself pushing & twisting
Open Oppen Poppen O O

o

&

nope it's not gonna stick I'll
need to keep it
mebbe try again

Unexploded Ordnance (UXO)

White Sands National Monument
White Sands Missile Range
New Mexico
Missile and Target Debris
Occasionally, missile malfunctions result in test debris outside Range boundaries. Some of these devices may be innocent looking metal boxes which actually contain explosives, flares, or detonators. Any of these items, as well as the antipersonnel bomblets, may explode if moved.
Explosives come in many shapes, sizes and colors. Some are hidden in electronic devices and other metal spheres which children might mistake for toy balls. Some are bright and shiny.

THE ORYX

What is the oryx?
The *Oryx gazella* is a large African antelope that now lives in southern New Mexico.
Why are they here?
The New Mexico department of game and fish wanted to establish a huntable big game population in an area where there were not currently huntable numbers of big game.
Why are the oryx so successful?
Their gestation period is 9 months. They are weaned at 3.5 months and by 5 months look like a small adult. They can reproduce at 2 years of age. Their life span is 20 years.

♪*we have come forth*♪
antiphony
strange noise ummhm
7 profets marching
throw the desert
♪*Joshua fit the battle of Jericho Jericho Jericho*
Joshua fit the battle of Jericho
& the walls come tumblin down♪
7 profits & 350 wives
hmm
joshua
legs apart
arms spread upwards
coyotefox as tree
I'll
wait here
until one a them wives
needs shade mmmhm
♪*and the walls come a-tumbling down*♪

one wife says look
at last a tree a hard tree
is good to find
& 350 wives
break off
his arms his legs
tonight we will have a fire

just a head
lickin holes where
limbs once were
rollin away
♪*we have come forth*
to prune the vineyard
prune the vineyard
for the last time♪

        And now I am prepared to say by
        the authority of Jesus Christ, that not

many years shall pass away before the United States shall present such a scene of *bloodshed* as has not a parallel in the history of our nation; pestilence, hail, famine, and earthquake will sweep the wicked of this generation from off the face of the land, to open and prepare the way for the return of the lost tribes of Israel from the north country. The people of the Lord, those who have complied with the requirements of the new covenant, have already commenced gathering together to Zion, which is in the state of Missouri; therefore I declare unto you the warning which the Lord has commanded to declare unto this generation, remembering that the eyes of my Maker are upon me, and that to him I am accountable for every word I say, wishing nothing worse to my fellow-men than their eternal salvation; therefore, "Fear God, and give glory to Him, for the hour of His judgment is come." Repent ye, repent ye, and embrace the everlasting covenant and flee to Zion, before the overflowing scourge overtake you, for there are those now living upon the earth whose eyes shall not be closed in death until they see all these things, which I have spoken, fulfilled

♪*for the last time till the next time*♪

When you see something that is technically sweet you go ahead and do it and you argue about what to do about it only after you have had your technical success. That's the way it was with the atomic bomb.

17

> The atomic bomb made the prospect of future war unendurable. It has led us up those last few steps to the mountain pass; and beyond there is a different country.

the grace in the ear

> **State of Samadhi**
> in prescribed duties; certainly; right; of you; never; in the fruits; at any time; never; in the result of the work; cause; become; never; of you; attachment; there should be; in not doing prescribed duties

> *no*
> You have a right to perform your prescribed duty, but you are not entitled to the fruits of action. Never consider yourself the cause of the results of your activities, and never be attached to not doing your duty.

so that person rolls
far away
sleeps awhile some
times he just sleeps
sometimes he sleeps &
snores sometimes that
person sleeps & dreams
of prophets

> DEAR BELOVED,

I am Sussan Adams

PLEASE ENDEAVOUR TO USE IT FOR THE CHILDREN OF GOD. I am the above named person. I am married to Dr. Donald Adams A LIBERIAN but I am now in Nigerian General HOSPITAL taking treatment for my sickness, who worked with U.S Embassy in LIBERIAN for nine years before he died in the year 2000..

When my late husband was alive he deposited the sum of $10.5 Million (Ten Million five hundred thousand U.S. Dollars) with A Bank Presently, this money is still under the safe keeping of the Reserve FINANCE COMPANY [ ]of the lord. Exodus 14 VS 14 says that the lord will fight my case and I shall hold my peace. I don't need any telephone communication in this regard because of my health because

wakes steals a lot
stuff
scraps of fur stuck
to cactus
someone's missal
sorry missile
bright & shiny
someone's knickers
too much stuff
hirples off going &

Fat Man *(10,800lbs)* Prints Available Sale Or Download HERE

I lost 80lbs To Become Ms Bikini America

How Do Celebs Look So Slim And Gorgeous?
Colonic Irrigation!

eating ordnance
breaks wind

every fart a crater dust
spirals away

CURRENT THREAT STATUS
SUBSTANTIAL

CONSTANT VIGILANCE
IS REQUIRED

SANDSTORM AREA FOR 2 MLS

♪Well now, God told Elijah, he would send down fire, send down fire from on high
He told the brother Noah by the rainbow sign, there'll be no water, but fire in the sky
Now don't get worried, just bear in mind, seek King Jesus and you shall find
Peace, happiness, and joy divine, with my Jesus in your mind

So, I say everybody's worried (yeah) 'bout the atomic bomb
But nobody's worried (no) 'bout the day

my Lord will come
When he'll hit, great God a-mighty,
like an atom bomb
When he comes, great God, when he comes♪

State of Utah, *downwind*
Ken's son was born in the Panguitch hospital. His face was a massive hole and they had to put all these pieces of his face back together. Ken could see down his throat, everything was just turned inside out, his face was curled out.

GUSTY WINDS MAY EXIST

There isn't anybody in the United States who isn't a down winder, either. When we followed the clouds, we went all over the United States from east to west and covering a broad spectrum of Mexico and Canada. Where are you going to draw the line? Everyone is a down winder. It circles the earth, round and round

well they always 're
going on about saviours
& all is well &
all shall be well & all shall be well
& all manner of thing shall be well
well well
think I'll try a prayer too
sez

break blow burn batter my heart
& fry it
now I am done amen
run like wind

whisky at night
water gallons by day just
to keep going
needs a piss unzips
lets out a stream to
sand dune floor
& stinkbug wakes up stinking
home flooded
spits a mouthful herself
her words run up piss river
nip & sting & burn
inside that person
's dick
fall to's scrotum
mutter & tell tales & argue
scritch

    Then we saw this tidal wave of dirt and dust and sagebrush and rattlesnakes and wires coming after us, it could have been any damn thing out there

dogcoyote wants
to know
are you now or
have you ever been a roadrunner

to know
why you're testing bombs

to see if they work
& picks up his arms
& his legs & his head
& walks away

          O Lord, You are as You have said, yet I wish to see Your divine cosmic form, O Supreme Being

          If the splendour of thousands of suns were to blaze forth all at once in the sky, even that would not resemble the splendor of that exalted being

          It's really quiet – as still as death – and then this real bright light for a few seconds. It was so bright I had my hands over my eyes closed, and I could see all these bones like you were looking at an X-ray

          a blinding flash lighting up the whole area brighter than the brightest daylight. A mountain range three miles from the observation point stood out in bold relief

          The brilliant light from the detonation pierced the early morning skies with such intensity that residents from a faraway neighboring community would swear that the sun came up twice that day.

          You would see the whole sky light up as if the sun were coming up backwards, and even the shadows of the trees would be wrong, casting their shadow in the other direction. And I should have known then that the world was upside down

First of all, when the bomb went off the light was like a thousand suns

SE FUE LA AZUCAR †

GENE MESSER

desert night
cold getting colder
what a fire coyote
fox makes sage
brush & mesquite

pretty soon fire
wood's gone coy

otefox thinks she thinks
pulls off a leg & flames bite
the fire blazes an

arm another leg
blazes pretty
soon only
's two eyeballs & a hole
left watching
glazed on desert sand

what's a sile-na-gig doing here

BEWARE OF RATTLESNAKES

> Coyote Dog Fox Hyena Jackal Wolf
> Cat Pig Lion Ass Donkey Horse Mule
> Armadillo Badger Bear Beaver Elephant
> Groundhog Hare Mole Mouse Muskrat
> Opossum Porcupine Rabbit Raccoon
> Rat Skunk Slug Snail Squirrel Worm
> Albatross Bat Bittern Buzzard Condor
> Coot Cormorant Crane Crow Cuckoo
> Eagle Flamingo Grebe Grosbeak Gull
> Hawk Heron Kite Lapwing Loon
> Magpie Osprey Owl Parrot Pelican
> Raven Roadrunner Sandpiper Seagull
> Stork Swallow Swift Vulture Water hen
> Woodpecker Alligator Crocodile Lizard
> Snake Turtle Blindworm Frog Newt
> Salamander Toad
>
> And all that have not fins and scales in the seas, and in the rivers, of all that move in the waters, and of any living thing which is in the waters, they shall be an abomination unto you
>
> Bullhead Catfish Eel Marlin Sturgeon
> Abalone Clam Crab Crayfish Lobster
> Mussel Prawn Oyster Scallop Shrimp
> Cuttlefish Jellyfish Limpet Octopus
> Squid Dolphin Otter Porpoise Seal
> Walrus Whale
>
> Jumbo was placed about 800 yards to the west of ground zero. Jumbo survived the test explosion intact.
>
> ♪Ya murió la cucaracha,
> Ya la llevan a enterrar,
> Entre cuatro zopilotes

25

Y un ratón de sacristan.♫

FLASH FLOODS

so this person
's caught in a bit of rain

call this rain
I remember when we all
were floating
even the loons & ducks couldn't
find mud for awhile

's how I made this place
with what they did find

seems to have dried a little

so that person himself
's talking to a mescalero
with enough chemicals
put em in the river
they'd poison all Tularosa
uhuh
drink he asks
named em by coming
into their houses
if one was making tortillas they'd
call him Tortilla
several Tortillas up there now
uhuh
great granma took in
Billy the Kid
a snotty nose
felt sorry for him

mmm sez
koyotefox
got the name no-one else
wanted

♪Cuando uno quiere a una
Y esta una no lo quiere,
Es lo mismo que si un calvo
En calle encuetr' un peine♪

♪Yo soy un hombre sincero
De donde crecen las palmas
Y antes de morirme quiero
Echar mis versos del alma♪

State of Dakota
they were going to
nail my hide to the barn door
they had me
under house arrest
they told me
what a traitor I was

State of California
they're the scoundrels
of the earth
struggling to make it
safe on paper
I wouldn't give you
two cents for any of them

State of California
I went to comb my hair
my scalp started to lift up
wouldn't trade my life
for a barrel of monkeys

                I'm not going to be worth
                a hill of beans
                remarkable thing
                he loves me anyway
                it sure makes me happy
                here I am fat, bald and toothless
                and he still loves me

ADOPT A HIGHWAY MILE

        Have you ever been arrested
    Or convicted for an offense or crime
          involving moral turpitude?

                ♪La cucaracha, la cucaracha,
                Ya no puede caminar;
                Porque no tiene, porque le falta
                Marijuana que fumar♪

coyotefox
sitting quiet
nothing in mind
cottonwood tree
small rustles
finally that person turns
noise is leaf people
tumbling
skittering along

the roadside
looks like fun sez
joins in mmm
hm
humvee 90 mph
thud splat
steamrollers coy
otefucked

the other people
dancing in the tailwind

                                ♪Hit the road Jack♪

picks 'sself up
shakes sez
some hit
need more of that
hangs
about the gas station
old cowboy driver
goes
for a piss
bathroom of all places

foxydog jumps in
hot holes
no
hotwires
brrroom & zoom &
squeal
gone

roadrunner dust
behind

                            ♪I'll make a cool hundred, I ain't got

time to stop for gas
I'll make a cool hundred, I ain't got
time to stop for gas
I'm gonna drive this automobile, just
as long as the gas lasts.♪

HIGHWAY 70

APACHE PICTURE SYMBOLS
CASINO OPENING

Mescalero Apache Reservation

FINGS LOTTERY GAMES
INTERNATIONAL
PROMOTIONS PROGRAMS

You have emerged as one of the winners of the FINGS-LOTTERY GAME INTERNATIONAL PROGRAMS. As a category (A) winner, you have been selected by computer balloting system where only email addresses are soughted, from a total numbers of 30,000 email addresses drawn from all over the globe. You have therefore been awarded a lump sum pay out of 2,000,000.00 **EUROS**.

. . . an abomination of Satan's handiwork . . .

thought this person'd
take off over the
Sacramento mntns
flying

waving to Badger
Bear
Lightning Rattle

Speech
Displaying Woman

Waving Person
all those old fellers
stars every one

HIGHWAY 54 ♪runs right by my baby's door♪

Three Rivers
bone dry

♪thigh bone's connected to the
hip bone
now hear the message of the
Lord♪

here's vineyards straight lines
irrigating Zinfandel
Chardonnay
Sangiovese
Merlot
Muscadet
mockingbirds
dessert

♪He who is thirsty
let him drink clear water♪

coffee in Tulie Sidewalk Café

Rowena Mac farms pistachios
down the road
bought some nuts

daughter runs it

she says
White Mountain
's called that
all year snow stayed
so deep   & she's 65
but now

says her daughter
rode horses
makes the best green chile &
apple pie

koi carp swimming here outside
speaking of water problems
seems Alamogordo
(synchronised spitting: fat aspens)
threw thorough
no through Federal Law
buys up
for city use
for flushing
60 thousand acres
's got 3 wells

right here alone's 20 thousand pistachio trees
white painted trunks
fruit of the desert

pie's on mum she says
won't take a $

                    FOR SALE
        40 ACRES PECAN TREES
        80 ACRES FARM LAND
        WELL WATER RIGHTS

Oscuro
even sand people
panting

Carriozo
hoohee
so fast overshoot
Coyote

                        ♪Oh, them dogs begin to bark,
                        hounds begin to howl
                        Oh, them dogs begin to bark,
                        hounds begin to howl
                        Oh, watch out strange kin people,
                        little red rooster's on the prowl♪

did it on purpose to
see what opossum
no
impostor
lives
here
set the dogs

                        ♪If you see my little red rooster,
                        please drag him on home
                        If you see my little red rooster,
                        please drag him on home
                        There ain't no peace in the barnyard
                        since my little red rooster's been gone♪

barking
back up back up
into Valley of Fires

                        ♪the Lord's my Shepherd I'll not
                                [missing]♪

where we would've
gone anyway for the
name alone
black lava folds
time collapses
on

HIGHWAY 380

Bingham
waving again
long dead miners
wobblies
unions of the states
woof warp salt of the

christ sz
Trinity

                                5:29.45 am Mountain War Time
                                July 16 1945
                                Typical radiation exposures for
                                Americans Per The National Council
                                on Radiation Protection
                                One hour at ground zero = ½ mrem
                                Cosmic rays from space = 40 mrem at
                                sea level per year
                                Although radiation levels are low, some feel any extra exposure should be avoided. The decision is yours. It should be noted that small children and pregnant women are potentially more at risk than the rest of the population and are generally considered groups who should only receive exposure in conjunction with medical diagnosis and treatment. Again, the choice is yours.
                                At ground zero, Trinitite, the green glassy substance found in the area, is still radioactive and must not be picked up.

& whofuck declares
war on mntns uh uh

                                Red Planet never closer than now

                                View of Mars will be stellar

                                If the Martians were to invade, now would be the time

here's the place
across the Rio Grande   ♪I'm an old cowhand
                                          Yippie yi yo kayah♪
San Antonio
carry us across   ♪One more river♪

INTERSTATE 25

San Marcial
nada & graves
all gone to meet their machair
no makar
the rest driven out by their
own desolation
disposable towns round
here

Elephant Butte Lake   Bear Beaver Elephant
                                          Groundhog Hare Krishna
                                          ♪I really want to see you Lord♪
40 miles of water   ♪Yippie yi yo♪
pissed in   ♪He who is thirsty♪

making leaves to dance

Redrock

Elephant Butte

Truth or Consequences
once was called Hot Springs
        but that's showbiz

himself once
had a visitor from
Unzen Jigoku in Japan
name of Kitsune-san
used to boil christians

in hot springs

better fried sz

think we'll play this game
settle in the Steak 'N Lobster Bar
faces to Turtle Ridge
drink Fat Tire beer
ask for the vegetarian menu
but shit get deep fried
battered
mush
rooms deep fried
battered courgettes deep
fried battered cauli
flowers &
a
smile

Fat Tire coyoteoldog
Fat Tire & a night's sleep

NO SOLICITORS

new day new
world thunderhead looming
clouds all worlds of

see a thousand miles
have we changed

no idea
how far we can
see
nose to the wheel
eyes mostly on the road

GUNS AND A MO

lost
in Fir St
Myrtle St
Radium St
morning cool
this is fine
we're here

                        DRIVING IN NEW MEXICO
                        Maximum speed 75 (auto) 75 (truck)
                        Right turn on red allowed

Williamsburg
population 527 elevation 4235
Las Palomas
resisting song but

                        ♪♪♪una paloma blancaaaa♪♪♪

Caballo &

                        ♪my wonderful wonderful four-legged
                        friend♪

HIGHWAY 187

Arrey
Derry
Garfield
Salem

                        in the s'd County on the 29th day of
                        June [torn] were Severaly arrigned on
                        Several Indictments for the horrible
                        Crime of Witchcraft by them practised
                        & Committed On Severall persons
                        [omitted] the 19th day for [torn] Instant
                        July between the houres of Eight &
                        [torn] in [torn] forenoon the same day

you Safely conduct the s'd Sarah Good Rebecka Nurse Sussan Martin Elizabeth Howe & Sarah Wild From thier Maj'ties goal in Salem afores'd to the place of Execution & there Cause them & Every of them to be hanged by the Neck untill they be dead [omitted] of the doings herein make return to the Clerke of the said Court & this precept and hereof you are not to fail at your perill and

To play Salem Witchcraft Trial Jeopardy, click on one of the dollar amounts below. An answer will appear. Try to provide the question that corresponds to that answer. Keep track of your score.

Mr. OUSMAN DABO.
AFRICAN DEVELOPMENT BANK (ADB)
OUAGADOUGOU BURKINA-FASO,
DearFriend,
I need your urgent assistance in transferring the sum of **($25.6 million)** to your account

FROM THE DESK OF AZZEM YARO.
BILL AND EXCHANGE MANAGER
BANK OF AFRICA (BOA)
OUAGADOUGOU, BURKINA FASO.
Dear friend,
This message might meet you in utmost surprise [deleted] opportunity of transfering the left over funds **$8.6 million** [ ] any foreign account.

Dear friend
I AM MR GORDO HASSAN [missing] ABANDONED SUM OF **($25,000,000.00)**.

Miles de amigos con tus mismas aficiones!

Hatch
chile capital of the world
30 thousand acres of chiles
no lima beans
a ballad of conquistadors

HIGHWAY 185

Rincon
Radium Springs
remember Geronimo
dunking here no
horses allowed
what was it called
before Radium before
Dona Ana
Fair Acres
Las Cruces &

careful of urinating
in holes
looking for a
*bath*room

climbing
back on

Or between 1933 & 1945
were you involved in any way in persecutions associated
with Nazi Germany or its allies?

HIGHWAY 70

not sure the old jalopy will
floorboarding
changing down
climbing
San Andres mountains
long haul

Organ
six thousand feets &
San Águstin Pass
smell of rain fat
drops come &
quickly going

clear to
White Sands Missile Park
150 miles Fat Tires all
the way
strictly 2 hours no
less

come nearly the full circle
thinking about the
old cowboy back at the
bathroom with gaspumps
scratching his head
know I left her here
someplace

so best
to walk into this Missile Park
cicadas singing zizzing
cops of two
different kinds everywhere
not so far for the old

feller to think he's
getting on a bit misplaced
his chevy just like
his glasses

                                      Honest John   Patriot   Little John
                                      Pogo Hi Terrier Corporal   Roland

                                      They are transportation systems, not simply a means of destruction, which can transport passengers or cargo across the depth of outer space equally as well as thermonuclear warheads between points on Earth

                                      Nestled away at various locations throughout the picturesque German countryside was a new weapon capable of mass destruction. This weapon was the V-2 rocket (*Vergeltungswaffe* or Vengeance Weapon.

                                      's mine said the Lord

                                      The V-2 rocket stood at 46.1 feet in length 65 inches in diameter, weighed over 27,000 pounds with a 2,200 pound payload and could travel 210 miles.

                                      This technological marvel was the brainchild of Dr Wernher von Braun.

so here's ironmongery
Lark Loon Falcon Hawk
Copperhead   Tartar
Athena Loki   Sly One   Shape Changer   Trickster
                                        Sky Traveller   Lie-Smith

Genie
dream of subtle fire

♪Dream a little dream of me♪

But those who swerve they are fuel for Hell-Fire

thou shalt not hearken unto the words of that dreamer of dreams for the Lord your God proveth you

IF IT FLIES IT DIES   "SCUD BUSTER"
FIRST TO FIRE

Corporal proving capital
tons heavy
surface to surface missiles
air to surface missiles
surface to air missiles
supersonic surface (sea) to air missiles
air to air missiles
Fat Man Bomb Casing

these highways
rulered straight across
deserts across rivers
boundaries at ninety
degrees

                               [omitted] intelligence and military services extricated Nazi scientists from Germany, during and after the final stages of World War II. Of particular interest were scientists specialising in aerodynamics and rocketry (such as those involved in the V-1 and V-2 projects), chemical weapons, [deleted] secretly brought to the United States, their service for Hitler's Third Reich,

> NSDAP and SS memberships as well as the classification of many as war criminals would have disqualified them from officially obtaining visas. The majority [torn] numbering almost 500, were deployed at White Sands Proving Ground, New Mexico; [deleted] to work on guided missile and ballistic missile technology. Much of the information surrounding Operation Paperclip is still classified.

in this park
where it should be
supermarket parking
slots for WMD
they're dropped just any
where wandering
organic glyph of missiles
end up shape of
the plumed serpent

koyotefox eyes fixing
each one to reuse
some way
trailer for old loon woman
water tank for duck girls
dog pen
mistle thrush

> Arthur Rudolph   Wernher von Braun   Kurt Blome   Herman Becker-Freysing Siegfried Ruff
> Klaus Barbie   Heinrich Rupp
> General Reinhard Gehlen
> Major General Walter Schreiber

but grins a little sz
this one

> SS11

wants to tuck it under
arm & run
this one'd
get stinkbug

> The LORD is a man of war: the
> LORD is his name.

in her hole

Sensitive Military Operations

talks to himself
don't mind
what people think
enjoys his own con
verse

seen enough need people
let's get out of here

tell me where there is
then we can
get out of here

going & again

smith of
brimstone engineer &
technician of collapsed lava

here's called hell
gypsum dunes
sun lives in the sand

                              Between 1945 and 1989, a total of
                              38,029 missile firings were completed
                              at WSMR (no later dates available)

but here's people I know
good old times
ugly ducklings

                              ♪Oh I would not exchange
                              my home on the range,
                              Where the deer and the antelope play;
                              Where seldom is heard
                              a discouraging word
                              And the skies are not cloudy all day.♪

going & never made
to stay except raising &
feeding the little ones

at home
straight a
way you do with old friends

sez evening
primrose
verbena
groundsel
rosemarymint
rice grass
hey that you sumac
all well Mormon tea
yucca my how you've grown

yucca says you would
this sand blowing
to your arm
pits

so going by dusk
out they come
movers
shakers all gone
Badger
Skunk
Rabbit
& Kit Fox
all a bit nervous
not seen himself
a while usually
ends a mess &
Stinkbug ready to hunker
down
spray coyotedog
skunky-wise
beg pardon Skunk

seems fair
Badger's sayin
how
'd it be if she
pissed & farted in your place
coyotedoggone messed up
your Isfahan rugs
shit in yer delft

SUPPLEMENTARY
INFORMATION
WSMR (White Sands Missile Range) covers approximately 3,200 mi\2\ of south-central New Mexico. Proposed DTRA activities at WSMR have the potential to significantly impact certain natural, social, cultural, and economic resources in the region. The study area for environmental analyses will include the

> Hard Target Defeat Test bed (HTDT), Permanent High Explosive Test Site (PHETS), Seismic Hardrock In Situ Test site (SHIST), Alternate SHIST, and Large Blast Thermal Simulator (LBTS). The objective will be to provide a thorough, comprehensive and PEIS for mitigation tracking concerning DTRA future activities. Significant Issues: Certain biologically diverse areas on White Sands Missile Range utilized by the Defense Threat Reduction Agency serve as habitat or potential habitat for protected floral and faunal (plant and animal) species.

hmm   hmm
how're you doing

so so but
every couple of hours
they throw ordnance at
us
come around sometimes
see how we're coping
how we get our
selves back together

lost my head once

not sure it's right now m

& they're all
crowding round
Spadefoot Kangaroorat Rabbit
Whiptail Skunk Old White Lizard
Night Hawk Sparrow Oriole
Roadrunner Roadrunner again

moving fast
even Transparent Cricket
Mockingbird mocking
a bit drunk that person

all speaking at once

or maybe just to yell at
some one

himself

sz don't see a problem
see what I cn do
see a person I know

more of a small depression

Dear Friend,
I need your urgent assistance.
Dear friend,
This message might meet you in
utmost surprise however, it's just my
urgent need (cut)
I NEED YOUR STRONG
ASSURANCE THAT YOU WILL
NEVER, NEVER CHEAT ME.
Dear Friend,
I guess this mail will find you in good
health and everything else ( )
Dear Friend,
Due to the sudden death of my
husband the former head of state
(omitted)
ATTN; Sir/Madam
With due respect, trust and humility

I write this letter to you (recently
murdered) as such I will be grateful
if you can assist us in this respect
(omitted)
Please treat this matter as very urgent.

State of California
hydrocephalic, misplaced rectum,
undescended testicle, atelectasis of the
lungs

State of Nevada
from the hips down legs all shrivelled
up & black; stem cell leukaemia

State of Utah
tumour the size of a large orange or
softball embedded in brain tissue

State of Nevada
some organs outside his body

State of Utah
little yellow ball with legs going out
like a spider

like that; that might be; effulgence; of
Him; the Great Lord

nowhere to go
so we go there
north
fast

RESPECT THE RATTLESNAKES PRIVACY

♪gonna find me a Mercury
cruise up and down the road♪

going &
trance driving
white gypsum desert
black lava desert

Laborcita
Luis Lopez
Socorro
Escondida
Lemitar
Chamizal
Polvadera
San Acacia
La Joya

east to Salinas
into the Manzano mntns
's ten
thousand foot purple
shadow
evening sun on
hills trees
become
moving animals
bunched cattle
black steers
freight train
cloudless sky
moving
not moving
transience

♪We'll raise up our glasses
Against evil forces
Singing, "Whiskey for my men,
beer for my horses!"
Take all the rope [missing]

Find a tall oak tree
Round up all of them bad boys
And hang 'em high in the street
For all the people to see♪

Abo Pueblo mission

Sixth. We are agreed as follows concerning the sword: The sword is ordained of God outside the perfection of Christ. It punishes and puts to death the wicked, and guards and protects the good. In the Law the sword was ordained for the punishment of the wicked and for their death, and the same [sword] is [now] ordained to be used by the worldly magistrates.

with kiva & altar
ruins
uneaten buffalo gourds
purple thistles'
thistles' shadows
juniper with red ribbons
dry creeks
cirrus

ammon mammon damn sz
Mennonites here
Church of
Belen
on the flood plain

ADOPT A BOULEVARD
SHRINES OF EL JEBEL

in the motel garden
blue carpet
27 bird boxes in the
maple
plastic frogs breeding
brooding childsize
flock of plastic
pink flamingoes
chickenwire stags
' nodding heads

hens duck ducklings
donkey & cart
small boys of plaster
aphrodite pours water under
bridges
lit with a thousand
lightbulbs
dogg in a manger

silver maple she says
has a sickness

setting sun
above
flocks & herds
Manzano's red
sandstone
soil
freight train mourns into
3am & stars
long river
undertow sleeps
motor pie
heart
      land dream
              ing

Immaculate War

having identified them to a moral certainty (a standard far short of what would be required by legal criteria of proof, it should be noted), there is no moral objection to targeting them. Indeed, one of the benefits of framing these operations as "war" rather than "law enforcement" is that it does not require the ideal outcome to be the apprehension and trial of the perpetrators. Instead, it countenances their direct elimination by military means

this's cat's cradle
cattycorner said here
Indra
's strings pull
the shutter's open time

This standard asks not what an individual knew, as a matter of fact, about a given situation or set of facts. Instead, it asks what a reasonable and prudent person in a similar situation should know. Thus, even if a person or government truthfully asserts that they were unaware of the activities of a terrorist cell in their territory, this does not provide moral immunity from attack. This standard asks not what they *did* know, but what they *ought to have known*

lapse
says
I don't know why govts lie

we cross
the autumn
in the larynx
not in things
not not in things
as one

with a caw
30 crows together
peel off the horse
chestnut tree
settle in a nearby
open book
flatten conjugate
solecize
this.
this.
this.

ethical warfare

time of geese skeins
all directions
flying low overhead
close yore mouth boy

riding the wave
when the shadow
of the turkey vulture
collides with that person's
cast ahead
crinkling over gravel
one vulturefox

descending sky

westing
past *2 Sticks Farm*
heat an
incoming tide rising from
that gravel

Jus in bello considerations
Attacks must be discriminate and they must be proportionate.

Military necessity permits actions that might otherwise be ethically questionable

audible
Painted Rock zoomorphs
anthropomorphs
vocables
motionless covered in
visible heat
Lizard Man
Turtle
Quail

                        Painted Rock Reservoir is closed to the public because it is one of the most toxic in the country with pesticide contamination. Its water will eventually disappear under the scorching summer sun, leaving behind a poisonous

tunnel from one world
to another
spiral into voicebox

unpracticed
rolling pebbles   Tohono O'odham
in a dry gullet   Hia Ced O'odham
those who have gone   Akimel O'odham

only insect voices
zing
Hohokam tongues   ghaan'ask'idii

NO WEAPONS OF ANY KIND
TO BE BROUGHT IN HERE

desert prune
old lady at *Gila Bend*

                                            Heloderma suspectum Gila monster is venomous heavy slow moving 2 feet long [torn] skin has the appearance of beads in the colors black pink orange yellow [deleted] intricate patterns

says her family escaped
dustbowl Oklahoma
to here
doctor wants to amputate
her injured foot
's not speaking
my language says

dull sullen thunder
no crackle anywhere but
fizz of lightning
splashes of heavy rain
Sonora desert monsoon

lean
45 degrees
sleep on air

                  HOT EATS COOL TREATS
                      NOW AVAILABLE
                GOD BLESS OUR TROOPS

between Gila Bend meandering

POISONOUS SNAKES AND INSECTS
INHABIT THE AREA

& *Buckeye*
anthropo zoo
pity the baking inmates
AZ State Penitentiary

          ♪Many days of sorrow,
          many nights of woe
          Many days of sorrow,
          many nights of woe
          And a ball and chain everywhere I go♪

3 wasps drinking
at the water fountain
patient

deep inside the yet to arrive
of arrow highways
desert pea gravel
swept to one line
raked labyrinth
this place

Salome
Euclid Avenue
colony strata left behind
at Gila Bend
10 000 acres green
irrigation from Colorado
River Aqueduct
mountains' ranges of hay
sight of water
dries kitdogfox tongue
into café fr coffee
single old men
church just out

middleaged women
waiting tables doing that
swerve dance

motel TV
climbing Eiger &
a man puts on shades
to see aliens
destroys em
zz sz himself

morning coffee with sugar
swerve step wait
ress café
French toast
w powder sugar mmm m

Health and happiness
are in your destiny
7 12 26 35 45 7

Yellow Bird Road
Little Road
wayside shrines
silkred
flowers
5 dead steers
in dark red
stain puddles
sun leathered hides
eyeholes   ♪Entre cuatro zopilotes
           Y un ratón de sacristan♪

Ak-Chin Indian Community President Taft [deleted] signed for a 47,600 acre reservation. [torn]

following year [bingo] he rescinded [torn] reduced the Community to just under 22,000 acres

water rights settlement approved by Congress in 1984, entitles the AK-Chin Community to 75,000 acre-feet of Colorado River water

casino is open 24 hours a day and has 475 slot machines, 40 poker tables and 500 bingo [bingo bingo] seats. It features a buffet restaurant and gift shop on the premises

**IRISH INDEPENDENT
HERITAGE TRUST FUNDS
87 Lisanally Lane
ARMAGH BT61 7HF
PIN No: 621280042CAM**
You have therefore been picked as the lucky owner of the PIN No [ ] designated amount of two Hundred & Fifty thousand, Nine Hundred & Fifty British Pounds Sterlings {**GBP £250,950.00**}.[bin][go]

waterless watercourse
Maricopa
coffee sugar
in Headquarters Café
old old feller says
'm so old
can't remember the last time
I remembered something
never havta worry about
running out of pills
anybody round here
seen old 2$ Alice

saguaro're mountains
too

wind

YOUR CAR WILL NOT RATTLE

                                      RECITAL
                                      Whereas, on December 7, 1941, the Imperial Japanese Navy and Air Force attacked units of the armed forces of the United States stationed at Pearl Harbor, Hawaii
                                      Whereas more than 2,000 citizens of the United States were killed and more than 1,000 citizens of the United States were wounded in the attack
                                      Whereas

whooohooo
all day driving
Pearl Harbor Highway
Radio Campesino   es mi gurra!   Mexicanissima!
                                            ♪Ay, ay, ay, ay,
                                          Ay, ay mi amor,
                                          Ay mi morena,
                                          De mi corazón.♪

range on range
receding
rising from desert
broken pins gap teeth
in ones threes
straight from floor to
foothills
whole horizons in

further in yet
though not green but
red ochre

not green by Lake Havasu
or along any stretch of Colorado
River

complete Fords
Chevies
whole trucks on high
steel poles
mechanics' shops
breakers' yards car
go cults   ♪riding along in my automobile
coming home to roost my baby beside me at the wheel♪

ADOPT A HIGHWAY
LAKE HAVASU CITY DESERT WALKERS

so cute
oilspill all
over mummy's knees
tahu ahu ahu haha
soon have him
walking
playing ball

ADOPT A HIGHWAY
INTERNATIONAL FOOTPRINT ASSOCIATION
CHAPTER # 476

La Paz County
Eagletail Mountains
Bighorn Mountains
Little H'arquhala Mountains
New Water Mountains
past *Hope*
Dome Rock Mountains
Plomosa Mountains
Buckskin Mountains
Mohave Mountains
Granite Wash Mountains

across route 66   ♪get your kicks♪

into Nevada   no corporate income tax, no personal income tax, no franchise tax, no inventory tax, no admissions tax, no unitary tax, no inheritance tax, no capital stock tax, is one reason many businesses are relocating to Nevada

Mojave dysart no
desrt
Colorado River Indian Reservation
Chemehuevi Indian Reservation
Fort Mohave Indian Reservation

not to Waba Yuma Peak
misread as
Wabi Yama
heavy eyes
o sad mountain

dogdog tired into
Searchlight
named after a fox *no*
box of matches
gas station woman

says gt gt granddaddy
founded the town
1897
George Frederick Colton

& pickup trucks with
saddles in the back
waiting

wild rue seeds in cofox
backsack may be soma

Indian Springs'
Moe's Casino
for breakfast pancakes coffee
feeding slots

himself
's enjoying the dance
kitchen cooks
waitresses
washers up
seamlessly moving fast
around each other
plates pots pans
head high on the swerve
on outstretched arm
smile & casual word

desert silence split
howling with jets from Nellis
Air Force Bombing and
Gunnery Range

mountains folded
lifted folded again

slowly walking
graceful
reds & ochres too

casual use
abandoned mines
deserted towns
ghosts gone	of the Mormon Battalion: Privates Allen, Rufus C. Allred, James R. Allred, James T. S. Allred, Reuben W. Beckstead, Gordon S. Beckstead, Orin M. Calkins, Alva C. Calkins, Edwin R. Calkins, James W. Calkins, Sylvanus. Decker, Zechariah [deleted] B. Hoyt, Henry P. Hoyt, [deleted] Timothy S. Kelley, Nicholas. Kelley, William. Sessions, John. Sessions, Richard. Sessions, William B. [del] Wriston, Isaac N. Wriston, John P. ♪*we have come forth we have come forth to prune*♪

mormons m
people of the dry book
latter day WMD every
one of em in
Mexican war	la intervención norteamericana
peace now thank christ
20 000 guns good ole boys
minutemen pa
trolling
that border whoda thought

drought clearances
another land over
the next range
always more land	those last few steps to the mountain pass; and beyond there is a different country

moving west

NEVADA TEST SITE
[deleted]
Jackass Yucca Frenchman Valleys
[deleted]
The Great Seal
of the State of Nevada

> a USDOE reservation near 3707N 11603W. Formerly known as the **Nevada Proving Ground**. [ ] for the testing of nuclear weapons, composed of approximately 1,350 square miles of desert and mountainous terrain. Nuclear testing began with a one-kiloton of TNT (4 terajoule) bomb dropped on Frenchman Flats on January 27, 1951.
>
> Porpoise Walrus Whale Turtle
> Blindworm Frog Newt Salamander
>
> **State of Utah to State of Nevada**
> you could see somewhere near where the blast was and it looked just like a tidal wave coming. The ground would go right to you, it was visible. The ground was moving, just like a wave in the water

Devil's Hole heat
's walking on razorblades
20 steps a minute says Tortoise
know what you mean

rocks walking
with wind
Amargosa Desert

How Many Toads Are There?
The Amargosa toad is considered voiceless

29$ motel
bar
ceiling stapled over
with bras
she's weeping
says 'm not a bad woman
2 husbands dead
2 divorced
Beatty
all change here for *Mercury*

gateway to the Test Site &
Yucca mntn

State of Nevada
I don't make a lot of noise. I don't know enough about what went on [ ] on the Test Site to give an educated opinion of what people should think. I don't think downwind has had any influence here, really

a ridge-line composed of volcanic material (mostly tuff) ejected from a now-extinct caldera-forming supervolcano

since 1976, there have been 621 seismic events of magnitude greater than 2.5 within a 50-mile radius of Yucca Mountain. [torn] [deleted] [missing] underground nuclear weapons tests at the Nevada Test Site have been excluded from this count

a reactive transport model is presented for the ambient hydrogeochemical system at Yucca Mountain (YM) [ ] simulates two-phase, nonisothermal, advective and diffusive flow and transport through one-dimensional matrix and fracture continua (dual permeability) containing ten kinetically reactive hydrostratigraphic layers. [ ] developed a thermodynamic interpretation of ambient groundwater chemistry at YM from limited analytical data and then combined it with insights from experimental and site-specific data to craft a conceptual model describing thermodynamic and kinetic relationships in the mineral/glass-water-gas system. The model was calibrated by adjusting uncertain thermodynamic and kinetic parameters to reflect observed trends at YM. The following calibration criteria were used to ensure that model predictions are consistent with hydrochemical and petrologic data from YM: (1) calculated multicomponent matrix pore water compositions do not vary significantly from reinterpreted analytical data; (2) simulated variations in matrix silica concentrations with depth are bounded by the observed analytical range; and (3) feldspars and glass dissolve while clays and calcite precipitate. The largest changes in calculated species concentrations occur in response to glass dissolution. Simulated matrix groundwater compositions at the depth of the potential repository are largely inherited from percolating waters rather than controlled by in situ chemical reactions. Predictions about groundwater flow pathways in the ambient YM system are sensitive to assumptions regarding percolation flux and fracture-matrix interactions. Confidence in complex reactive transport models of the thermally perturbed YM repository system depends on successful representation of ambient system conditions.

Desert Earthquake Hits Near Yucca Mountain No Injuries or Damage Reported

For Immediate Release: Friday, June 14, 2002
News Media Contact: Allen Benson, 702/794-1322 Yucca Mountain Project Office Statement on Nevada Earthquake Report:
There was not an earthquake at Yucca Mountain today

Nuclear weapons are useful because they are unusable.

Our potential enemies are burrowing in [ ] in hard and deeply buried bunkers

The Robust Nuclear Earth Penetrator program does not create a new nuclear weapon. It is only intended to explore whether you can encase a weapon in order to allow it to penetrate

dream eyes
wild burros here
always stepping on toad people
shplup
pin tails on em all heh heh
they like it m

before it explodes so that you can hold that target at risk and continue to deter the use of weapons of mass destruction

Deep Geological Repository: authorized storage of up to 70 000 metric tons of used nuclear fuel and high-level radioactive defense waste at the repository [ ] 120 000 metric tons could be stored safely at Yucca Mountain. Independent scientific studies concluded that the repository could be expanded to contain an even greater volume

at 1500 feet for 10 000 years

remember
10 000 yrs ago
& remember
10 000 yrs from now
here
no thought
sz well I haven't slept
for a while &
woo sz this person his
self
woo &
hoo

's away with
old friend plant people
been around
desert mariposa♪ ♪trampa que no mata
pero no libera
vivo muriendo prisionero
mariposa traicionera
todo se lo lleva el viento,
flower in flower   mariposa no regreso♪
open your thighs
century plant
mescal
tequila
sz

need a haircut
sz that person
trim & bath
screwdriver
bloody mary
martini shaken

then a drink

Or are you seeking entry to engage in criminal activity

so this San
Francisco eh hmm   ♪some gentle people there♪

looking for a good barber
there's a clean shaven gent
e'scuse me we sez

out of my way
'f I had my way
all you
street people wit no
gumption
t earn a living'd
be rounded up
kept on Alcatraz

why thankyou sir
you've opened my eyes
thanks I'll
clean up right away

boots cracked
blackness in pockets
hair full of sand
swing down
to the Pacific Ocean

it's not empty
our pockets are

but that
there's emptiness
in em

since noone cn leave
here
kitfox looking
back up hills
with burning in him swollen light
dark light of a diseased liver
his heart falls out
leaves it
leaves there

                                      as for coyot as for turtle the lie of raw
                                      materials one thing all bagfull and the
                                      disc which satisfy the half which the year
                                      white crow is red are blue was satisfied
                                      no

a whole bagfull
lies & tortoises
a red crow
half a year
the blue one of 12
white discs
stuff

                                      tidal wave of dirt and dust and sagebrush
                                      and   rattlesnakes, any damn thing out
                                      there

At [missing] Pacific Daylight Time on [torn] an earthquake with preliminary magnitude 4.0 occurred 75 miles west of S[deleted], California. The magnitude is such that a tsunami [ ] be generated. This will be the only WC/ATWC message issued for this event.
Further information will be issued by the United States Geological Survey

The ground would go right to you, it was visible. The ground was moving, just like a wave in the water

Senators say Terrorism not an Investment Opportunity

Our moral activities *no*
Or immoral activities

Or a violation related to a controlled substance

Or been arrested or convicted for two or more offenses for which the aggregate sentence to confinement was five years or more

Or been a controlled substance trafficker

**U.S presses program
for new atom bombs**

Pentagon is seeking weaponry to strike at adversaries buried deep in bunkers

This week, 10 minutes by car south of Omaha, Nebraska, the U.S. Strategic Command is holding a little-advertised meeting at which the Bush administration is to solidify its plans for acquiring a new generation of nuclear arms.

Topping the wish list are weapons meant to penetrate deep into the earth to destroy enemy bunkers. The Pentagon believes that more than 70 nations, big and small, now have some 1,400 underground command posts and sites for ballistic missiles and weapons of mass destruction.

Determined to fight fire with fire, the Defense Department wants bomb makers to develop a class of relatively small nuclear arms – ranging from a fraction the size of the Hiroshima bomb to several times as large – that could pierce rock and reinforced concrete and turn strongholds into radioactive dust.

[deleted] many buried targets could be attacked
[deleted] the administration said in its Nuclear Posture Review

wind that sky

                        this world turns

who attempts or advocates the over-throw of the Constitution of Japan or the Government formed there-under by means of force or violence, or who organizes or is a member of a political party or any other organization, which attempts or advocates the same

           stuff in his bag
           alarm clock in his chest
           where's heart sat
           not liking the cut
           of this jib the sound

violation of the provisions of Paragraph 1 (excluding Item (6)) to Paragraph 3 of Article 23 of the Passport Law (Law No. 267 of 1951). [vanished] punished for violation of the provisions of Article 74 to 74-6-3, or 74-8.

           of this & sure
           's wearing a suit natty
           charcoal grey old style
           with chrys
           anthemum buttonhole person
           complaining time to time of thirst
           's taken the advice of the nice gent
           but's not short of nous
           knows that to climb a stair at night
           step at the edges or
           creak
           & clean clipped
           but hmmm
           when

♪Natty Dread rides again♪   he smiles teeth're pretty
           fierce
           tongue stick out a little
           eye a bit red
           maybe not that iris that were
           scanned
           & since shit happens
           now ties his head on
           could be turban
           just shaved whiskers
           all pale there
           's got undeclared nail

clippers
& christ the spare pen
etrator's
in the
still got stinkbug's arse
hole spose they probe
with all their questions
the bag the bag
's full of
stuff stolen

the Narcotics and Psychotropic [rip] lies Substances Control Law, the Marijuana Control Law, the Opium Law, the Stimulants Control Law, the Law Concerning Special Provisions for the Narcotics and Psychotropics Control Law, etc. and Other Matters for the Prevention of Activities Encouraging Illicit Conducts and Other Activities Involving Controlled Substances through International Co-operation (Law No.94 of 1991) or Book II, Chapter XIV of the Penal Code (Law No.45 of 1907).

uh oh
& shit what the hell
's my name fuck
don't want to be
caught
little ratón in a trap no
going & going
going & staying
going & being
being & becoming
telephone box job

in a trice

Is it a bird? Is it a plane? *No*

♪La cucaracha la cucaracha
Ya no puede caminar
Porque no tiene, porque le falta
Legalidad por entrar♪

♪watch out little red rooster
strange kin people on the prowl♪

                                    cocka cockahoop
                                    cockatiel cockerel no

                                    kitcockaroach
                                    looking fr a tasty apple
                                    boss
                                    speedy motormoving
                                    right enough
                                    's past immigration
                                    coming to the customs
                                    past customs speeding sideyways
                                    unseen scuttle
                                    fish clear to clean air
                                    well carpark air
                                    bit damp & muggy
                                    looks up for sun &

                                    cracklesplat crunch oh
                                    fuck Toyota Land
                                    cruiser

punished for violation of the provisions
of Paragraph 1 (Law No.45 of 1907).

                                    black deep
                                    how long's time

                                    doesn't pay

                                    chitin himself
                                    peel up
                                    roll to shade
                                    old ginkgo tree

with what's dropped
dumped
bent beercan
old bone apple
core
grist
matter
immanence
refashions's trunk
legs arms
iridescent
cicada wings fr eyes
's nearly good as new
little thirsty though
Flat Tire
mmm

gon gon
harrrumph
goin & going

not a cloud in the sky
hurrying

kitkot sez
think we cn walk quiet here
& if we can't
hop a bullet

stroll into town
touaregs no no
tourists
dream to dream
bim bam

　　　　　　　　　　　　don don round the corner don bam
　　　　　　　　　　　　million people hulla
　　　　　　　　　　　　baloo don don
　　　　　　　　　　　　yelling eating children
　　　　　　　　　　　　drinking corners pushing
　　　　　　　　　　　　loin
　　　　　　　　　　　　cloths running with jayz that's
　　　　　　　　　　　　got to weigh a ton &
　　　　　　　　　　　　thirty of em hefting
　　　　　　　　　　　　running
　　　　　　　　　　　　60 twinkling legs under
　　　　　　　　　　　　yellow red blue green mountain
　　　　　　　　　　　　painted carved leering
　　　　　　　　　　　　's a float
　　　　　　　　　　　　with hare
　　　　　　　　　　　　on a shark
　　　　　　　　　　　　don't believe Hare
　　　　　　　　　　　　every where
　　　　　　　　　　　　wine
　　　　　　　　　　　　2 million hands throwing water
　　　　　　　　　　　　sweet rain wine
　　　　　　　　　　　　get some of that
　　　　　　　　　　　　hooraying himself loves
　　　　　　　　　　　　a parade paroompah
　　　　　　　　　　　　oompah
　　　　　　　　　　　　's playing trombone
　　　　　　　　　　　　with wine bottle crows
　　　　　　　　　　　　cicadas wine
　　　　　　　　　　　　icecream wine children gawping
　　　　　　　　　　　　legs hopping jamming
　　　　　　　　　　　　the place til
　　　　　　　　　　　　drop wine down drunk

Porpoise Walrus　　　　　　　grampus hotel
　　　　　　　　　　　　room
　　　　　　　　　　　　that person

                                      recognise as
                                      isosceles triangle
                                      which angle has the
                                      o christ
                                      bathroom
                                      tv
                                      eating contest must
                                      beat 58 hotdogs
                                      10 minutes
                                      fold em in half
                                      's the trick &
                                      swallow
                                      bathroom rush
                                      zz

                                      woken by cicadas roaring
                                      chose the wrong head
                                      's broken
                                      dogfur mouth sz
                                      going &

                                      trees with paper wishes tied
                                      ginkgo growing old with banana

sick on a journey   fortune teller from Manchuria says
dreams wandering   they raped em all
                                        they did not have human faces
                                      & the nation sliding down

                                      prefer the health & happiness
                                      routine
                                      going

where's shade
great—coming—from—sunlight—
buddha here
50 feet high
3 foot eye
bits
burned bits saved burned
again
head of estuary
hands of peachboy mntn
one held up

know how he feels
that person sz

's guardians
thunderfaced
one forever uttering
the other muttering
ah un
ah om
alpha omega

himself mumbles
history
camped here long
enough
let's visit the deer folk
believe we have friends in common
past

wild straight pines
heron preening
cicadas humveeing sound &

what's that stink

face clenched ah
few
's deer piss

and *you* are says a big buck
you'd better polite ok we
're messengers of the gods
mmmhm sez that person
what about person
al hygiene
listen shorty says buck
there's eleven hundred of us here
not much space right & the baldy
fellers don't help
fugue & shambling about
mumbling ah & lotus &
gone beyond & blah
we can't get beyond the f fuf
fence ok
only fun here
's to knock over small kids ok
steal their food
rub up to lovely soft people
piss suddenly shd see their
faces hon hon hon
batteries not included ok
gimme that hi jean stuff
name's sika
and *you* are

himself
's off
pissing can be
dangerous
but's saying
messengers of the pish
I'm

                              summoner of kingfishers
                              the one geese kiss
                              the one with 5 & 9 tails
                              old compound eye
                              the one chestnuts fall for
                              the one in sunshafts clipping grapes
                              with broken scissors
                              bringer of acorns
                              fat with mushrooms
                              drinker of aftershock
                              the squeaky clean one
                              frogvoice
                              the one wit no flies on
♪Fireflies, Fireflies   uh
Drink sake in a brewery

                              huh
                              'm hungry
                              fried beancurd tonight
                              wine
                              m
                              but fr now
                              frothy tea
                              brackenroot sweets
                              watching
Come down Fireflies   dragonflies jink turn
Come down, come down.♪   on the spot
                              world go by

                              open hands
                              why does this heron not
                              eat the carp

                              cicada dragging along
                              burst intestines

cockroach in my boot poor dearie
just looking for a meal

she smiles going one way
smiles again returning
raises her hand

now

pointing
some of that
long radish
food arrives on the table
with wine beer tea
lotusroot dumplings
yuba soup
fried beancurd
steamed beancurd
beancurd in buckwheat noodles
wine
cream with arrowroot
sticky rice
horseradish hoooo
beer beer
square dishes with holes
fanshape dishes with lids
gourdcurve dishes
little wine cups
keep filling
emselves
filling
stuff yer deepfried
random memory

filling

rolling & rolling
street man

                        face bunched
                        armsweeps across
                        chest
                        again
                        face bunching each time
                        himself hands
                        over half full bottle
                        may his beard unmat
                        his feet clean
                        sleep sound in
                        fine linen untroubled

♪Gin a body meet a body
Comin thro the rye♪

                        bats & barbed
                        wire hangover
                        green man tune at crossings

                        too loud
                        burns synapses
                        swerve from sun
                        sidestreet templegarden
                        kind stranger
                        sitting smoking
                        Mr Hara
                        says
                        not to eat that fruit
                        even if
                        thirsty
                        used for making hair oil
                        Mrs Shimura
                        not smoking says kindly
                        famous painter lived here

They seem to think
my studio's a kind of toilet
they each come
with a roll of paper

come tomorrow for tea
tonight watch candles

turtles with red eye stripes
smart
above water only heads
size of dinner plates
butterflies saucer size
size of's eyes
eyes size of thirst
throat croak
heron & that person
startle each other
she's staring at her
own reflection
waiting to eat reverie

off to isosceles
dream of pi
3.1415926535897932384626433
on's tomb
stone
π

♪don don su don don don♪

drums pound
out of bed
conch hoots
cicadas boombassing
run for tea
drouth endures
Mrs Shimura
's arranged lotus
tea's made
offered
to boss Eisai
dead 900 years

glottal chants from
that elder world

at heart of mself's
daily wheel round
bald monks prostrate
walk formula in
serpent line
bow 9 times leaving
basket headed flute
players
playing
on

still clinging
to trees pillars
cicadas' husks
shrugged & wriggled
off

inch
worms
pomegranates
hang

There are those who see water as beautiful flowers; but they don't use flowers as water.

gon & going
been there
here they caught a mermaid
called the place Sea God's Temple

buried her here

nowhere slowly
this ginkgo alive

♪What a beautiful tree
Kushida's ginkgo!
Twigs grow to branches
Young leaves become a thicket♪

                        as long as Eisai
                        's dead

                        shifted space
                        the hole to climb through

7.30am
                        at the beginning
                        anonymous
                        no eyes
                        turned on him
                        little tambours drummed
                        with small paddles
                        four even beats
                        three close together
                        & again
                        yellow robes
                        in front of the dome
                        grey ponytails
                        monks children coiffed women
                        thick keloid scar tissue
                        bent backs
                        bald monks
                        nuns businessmen
                        bagladies toddlers
                        bondondon &
                        again
                        sitting
                        teddy bear blankets

Atomic Bomb Dome

8.00am

Dedication of the Register of the Names of the Fallen Atomic Bomb Victims
Eligible victims
[   ] **Directly exposed** [   ] **Exposed** [   ] **Affected** [   ] **Exposed in their mothers' wombs**.

number of names in the Register was 237,062 [missing] the bones of another estimated 85 persons were unearthed on Ninoshima Island in in Hiroshima Bay

Bomb Memorial Mound [ ] contains the identified but unclaimed remains of 831 persons and the unidentified remains of roughly 70,000

617 victims unearthed

216 bodies, 156 cremated [ ] 60 simply abandoned on the grassy field

on blue tarps' congruity
before world
seeing right through

shifting ebbing going
& staying
restless still
within
starling's fluid flights
silver darling shoals
small swirl of
humans'

here's world

tongue swallowed
hand to ear

the other shading eyes'
clear blue sky
signals

Thus I have heard   is

he reached down and took a woman
by the hands but her skin slipped off
in glovelike pieces

a naked living woman burned from
head to toe

only medicine was iodine
everything he had painted now has
pus on it

their mouths swollen pus-covered
wounds

their faces were wholly burned
their eye sockets were hollow
fluid from their melted eyes had run
down their cheeks

                                        mself
                                        a shadow
                                        turning
                                        mothers daughters
                                        aunties cousins
                                        illicit lovers' lips & napes

                                        flesh flower branded
                                        through clothes' patterns

                                        gravel melted to glass

                                        no there here
                                        then now

8.06am   empty chair rows
                                        yellow chrysanthemum rows

Dedication of Flowers

                    it was said
For seventy five years nothing will grow
New buds sprouted
In the green that came back to life   drinks it thirsty
                                                    tears pus
                                                  a field for ashes' shoots
                                                  epicentre's aloe yucca
                                                  sickle senna
                                                  panic grass
                                                  feverfew
                                                  clotbur
                                                  sesame
                                                  hairy-fruited bean
                                                  purslane
                                                  bluets
                                                  goosefoot
                                                  morning glories
                                                  day lilies

8.15am   measuring time

8.16am
Declaration   doves' crackling wings
                                                  yellow chrysanthemum rows
                                                  white chrysanthemum rows
                                                  bestiaries breviaries of rows
                                                  of bunches of flowers
                                                  charged with alphabets' babel
                                                  sounded petals' annual
                                                  biennial

perennial
one sun's
enough

8.23am
Commitment

8.24
8.25
8.26
8.27

one sun

incense burning rows

blue skies'
half moon

mslf
breathes
cicadas zisz
one again sun

long lines of refugees, just quiet, I don't know why they were so quiet [missing] like ghosts [deleted] stretching out their arms because the skin was peeling off from the tips of their fingers. I could clearly see the hanging skin, peeling skin, and the wet red flesh and their hair was burned and smelled, the burnt hair smelled a lot [ ] just slowly passed by the front of my house. I brought them water. They thanked me but some of them were drinking water and vomiting blood and [then] died, stopped moving. They died in front of me. I felt regret and so scared. Maybe I killed them? Did I kill them?

dying mysteriously and horribly—people who were uninjured (even) in the cataclysm—from an unknown something [deleted] atomic

U.S. authorities responded in time-honored fashion: [deleted] attacked the messenger [deleted] expelled from Japan [ ] camera vanished [ ] accused [torn] influenced by Japanese propaganda [ ] scoffed at (the notion of) an atomic sickness
U.S military press release right after the bombing downplayed human

U.S. ATOM BOMB SITE BELIES TOKYO TALES: TESTS ON NEW MEXICO RANGE CONFIRM THAT BLAST AND NOT RADIATION TOOK TOLL

historic ground in New Mexico, scene of the first atomic explosion on earth and cradle of a new era in civilization, gave the most effective answer today to Japanese propaganda that radiations [sic][ ] were responsible for deaths even after the day of the explosion, Aug. 6, and that persons entering Hiroshima had contracted mysterious maladies due to persistent radioactivity

**NO RADIOACTIVITY
IN HIROSHIMA RUIN**

US scientist who watched the first atomic bomb blast and campaigned for arms control (obit)
[protégé of Oppenheimer] assembled core for Fat Man bomb dropped on

Nagasaki [ ] I am completely convinced another war cannot be allowed [deleted] under investigation [ ] 45 years later accused of being a spy

No effort was made, and none was seriously considered to achieve surrender merely in order not to have to use the bomb

11.00am

in the morning of August 9 Prime Minister Kintaro Suzuki addressed the Japanese Cabinet [ ] [ ] terminate the war

Nevada Test Site [ ] cyclone-fence pens hold protesters Military police, tired of the caging, bused a group of arrestees 60 miles out into the desert, [deleted] and drove off

Protest as Terrorism
[ ] threat of terrorism toward the Nevada Nuclear Test Site and the proposed Yucca Mountain Nuclear Waste Repository by domestic protest groups [deleted] particularly anti-nuclear activists

spiralling doric cyclone
syzygy twister that person
epicentre's yucca
panic grass

Costs of the Manhattan Project
figures in constant dollars
Expenditures through August 1945:*
*Includes costs from 1940-42 for the National Defense Research Council and the Office of Scientific Research and Development. Excludes $76 million spent by the Army Air Forces on Project SILVERPLATE from September 1943 through September 1945 (SILVERPLATE covered the modification of 46 B-29 bombers in support of Manhattan Project, trained personnel of 509th composite bombing group, provided logistical support for units based at Tinian Island, launching point for the attacks on Japan)

$20 billion

    behind this hedge
    stacked rakes

    along the river floating
    paper lanterns

    well water
    reflecting leaves

    round the tree rows
    dusk

    alone
    on the mountain

    since the womb
    climbing

    red wooden gateway
    yellow endgrain

    cobwebs' spiders'
    munitions case shrine

                                        another's cement's
                                        dome shaped

                                        inside boulder fissure
                                        8 round stones' shrine

                                        mountainside's
                                        stupa inside

                                        sakyamuni's ashes
                                        ten thousand thousand stones

                                        each being borne
                                        by Hiroshima folk

                                        cricket cleaning
                                        her mandibles
Things about which one is liable to be negligent day flowers
Things that especially attract one's attention   oyster mushrooms
Things that give a clean feeling   ceps
Things that arouse a fond memory of the past   red eyestripe turtle
Things that arrest about a lover's face   heron
                                        & other people
                                        who do not go to war

Things that are at odds with nature
Things that fall from the sky

                                        in these wards
                                        Ogon mountain
                                        Futaba mountain
                                        Ushita mountain
                                        Chausu mountain
                                        Suzugamine mountain
                                        maple
                                        pine
                                        camellia

[torn]
[omitted]
[deleted]

11.00am

in the morning of August 9 Prime Minister Kintaro Suzuki addressed the Japanese Cabinet [   ]

11.02am

cherry
looking
on

one bluish white
bluish red
white
greenish yellow sun

so strong that all living beings had been turned to powder
there were no corpses to be seen

as if blue morning-glories had suddenly bloomed up in the sky.
They were bleeding all over and some of them had no clothes. Many of them were carrying people on their shoulders.
The city turned into the colour of the yellow desert.

it was like being roasted alive many times over. It was terribly hot, much worse than the pain which one must endure when an incision is made during surgery. I could see people running in the dark. Some of them were on fire, then, the sun ray broke through the clouds. The light appeared to be in many different colors, red and yellow, purple and also white.

just dug out red soil and roof tiles to help my family; my mother, my three sisters and a child of one of my sisters. The river was also filled with dead people blown by the blast and with survivors who came here to seek water. Anyway I could not see the surface of the water at all.

We took care of the people around us by using the clothes of dead people as bandages, especially for those who were terribly wounded.

I crossed Matsuyama Bridge over Shimonokawa. There were so many human corpses under it that they formed a dam in the stream

[ ] the smell human beings produce when they are burned is the same as that of the dried squid when it is grilled. The squid – we like so much to eat. When I felt someone touch my leg, it was a pregnant woman. She said that she was about to die in a few hours. She said, "I know that I am going to die. But I can feel that my baby is moving inside. It wants to get out of the room. I don't mind if I die. But if the baby is delivered now, it does not have to die with me".

classmates lying alive. I held him up in my arms [ ] his skull was cracked open, his flesh was dangling out from his head. He had only one eye left, and it was looking right at me. [ ] I could hear him crying out, "Mother, Mother" [ ] he told me to go away.

The water was dead people. I had to push the bodies aside to drink the muddy water

I put my handkerchief in the water and I put it over her burns, but she went on crying in pain.

all the cries of the students for help and for their mothers. It just didn't stop

wished I had died with my sisters.

it began to rain. The fire and the smoke made us so thirsty and there was nothing to drink, no water. As it began to rain, people opened their mouths and turned their faces towards the sky and tried to drink the rain, but it wasn't easy to catch the rain drops in our mouths. It was a black rain with big drops.
They were so big that we even felt pain when they dropped onto us. We opened our mouths just like this, as wide as possible in an effort to quench our thirst. I felt [ ] was entirely covered with only three colors. I remember red, black and brown, but, but, nothing else.
[ ] The fingertips of those dead bodies caught fire and the fire gradually spread over their entire bodies from their fingers. A light gray liquid dripped down their hands, scorching their fingers. I, I was so shocked to know that fingers and bodies could be burned and deformed like that, [ ] hands and fingers that would hold babies or turn pages, they just, they just burned away.

her skin was just peeling right off. The maggots were coming out all over. I couldn't wipe them off. I thought it would be too painful. I picked off some maggots, though. And nine hours later, she died [   ] on my lap [ ] she said, "I don't want to die." I told her, "Hang on Hang on." She said, "I won't die before my brother comes home." But she was in pain and she kept crying, "Brother. Mother."

I joined the white chrysanthemum organization, pledging to donate my body upon death for medical education and research. My registration number is number 1200. I'm ready.

I held him firmly and looked down on him. He had been standing by the window and I think fragments of glass had pierced his head. His face was a mess because of the blood flowing from his head. But he looked at my face and smiled. His smile has remained glued in my memory. He did not comprehend what had happened. And so he looked at me and smiled at my face which was all bloody. I had plenty of milk which he drank all throughout that day. I think my child sucked the poison right out of my body. And soon after that he died. Yes, I think that he died for me.

and a woman whose eye balls were sticking out. Her whole baby was bleeding.

A mother and her baby were lying with skin completely peeled off.

another friend of mine, I wondered why the soles of his feet were badly burnt [ ] it was undeniable fact the soles were peeling and red muscle was exposed. Even I myself was terribly burnt, I could not go home ignoring him. I made him crawl using his arms and knees. Next, I made him stand on his heels and I supported him. We walked heading toward my home repeating the two methods. When we were resting because we were so exhausted, I found my grandfather's brother and his wife, in other words, great uncle and great aunt, coming toward us [ ] [they] seemed to be Buddhas wandering in living hell

They were helping each other. But they were barely making their way. I cried [ ] these were mounds. If I tried to find my beloved ones, I would have to remove the bodies one by one. There were all kinds of bodies in the mounds. Not only human bodies but bodies of birds, cats and dogs and even that of a cow. I can't find words to describe it. They were burned, just like human bodies, and some of them were half burnt. There was even a swollen horse. Just everything was there, everything.

How, how can I say it?

da**fa** da**fa** da**fa**

dahfoo dahfoo dahfoo
she names each stone
on the bridge with her
small girl hand
himself going
opposite direction
long nose pretty
fierce teeth not
kempt smiles
inclines head

dahfoo smiles back
passes by
neither going

with dahfoo
's mother
three more people who
do not go

between coming &
going
a fully awake world
's native land
mntns & waters here
to here
sweet in
belly

Inasa mountain
Nishizake mountain
Unzen
Fugen mountain
Heisei Shinzan

further in
eagles wheeling
birds outsing cicadas
farmland
ducks with hens
sows
herbs hanging to
kindly wind & sun
oranges lemons
purpling figs
apples
squash
these
persimmons
're small
saplings grown
from bombed tree
seeds
Dr Ebinuma
's saying pausing
from spraying
smoking we
pluck figs from limbs
eat apples water
melon
slices' everywhere juice
on's whiskers
a moment's
serious laughing
matter
the toad that was
squatting
on
's liver's
hopped
off
greened hills'
going

& ah
dayflower
riverbank garlic
flea bane
creeping wood sorrel
fartsmell flower
awake fool's plant

St Paul Parking

♪I see sparks before my eyes
Or is it stars up in the skies
Oh yes, I have that funny feeling♪

his polished motorcycle
's tempting to shoplift
trembling thighs
going & going
peach nipples &
luculent gaze
easy up to snow
ice grabbing
goosewings
argue with north
arrive together
in that hot early world

hungry
's not a monk
so
fish
's a vegetable

♪Come down Fireflies♪

        Junko's saying &
        octopus squid
        a delicacy Hitomi
        says this's pig's
        cartilage mm m
        call for
        buckwheat
        beancurd
        fermented soybean
        dumplings
        wine spins cup
        to cup
        beer's for thirst

        first food was
        apples before I tasted
        anything
        rice scarce
        even born 4 years after
        the sun burst
        Ebinuma's saying

        noses angle
        to cups again
        heads in mountains'
        trailing clouds

        talk's in the fruit of trees
        cedar's smell
        mountains' hermits'
        waterfilled grapes
        cicada sounds striking rock's heart
        & thrift's gone late wine
        we're in that land tickling
        carp & cuddling trout *no*
        the other way

in stone's wave
night's still there
heron's darkness hunched
stars' noise silences
himself drink too much
air

Credits

I have quoted from the following books:

Carole Gallagher. *American Ground Zero: The Secret Nuclear War*. Boston: The MIT Press 1982.
Bhagavad Gita; ed. His Divine Grace AC Bhaktivedanta Swami Prabhupada, International Society for Krishna Consciousness 1983, (as well as Ramanand Prasad's American Geeta version)
Dogen Kigen. *Shobogenzo* (1240)
John Hersey. *Hiroshima*. Harmondsworth: Penguin Books, 1946
Sei Shonagon, *The Pillow Book of Sei Shonagon* (996)
Nagasaki Journey: The Photographs of Yosuke Yamahata, August 10 1945. Pomegranate Artbooks 1995
Hibakusha ; Nihon Hidankyo (nd)
The Bible (Leviticus, Deutoronomy, Exodus & psalm 23)
The Qu'uran

the newspapers & periodicals:

USA Today; Dan Vergan reporting July 14th, 2003.
Daily Express; 'The Atomic Plague' by Wilfred Burchett, Sept 5, 1945.
New York Times; William L Laurence, Sept 12, 1945.
The Guardian; Michael Carrison, April 27, 2005.
Oakland Tribune, 31st July, 2003
International Herald Tribune / Asahi Shimbun; August 4, 2003.
AP release; Ken Ritter, June 14, 2002.
Ethics & International Affairs 14 (2000); 'Immaculate War' by Martin L Cook
'Ethical Issues in Counterterrorism Warfare'; Martin L Cook
Computers & Geosciences vol 29 issue 3 2003; 'Reactive transport model for the ambient unsaturated hydrogeochemical system at Yucca Mountain' (abstract)
American Behavioral Scientist vol 46 745–765, 2003; Robert Futrell, Barbara G Brents

the BBC interview: August 1945, 2005, Keiko Ogura.

the leaflets:

Ak Chin Comunity leaflet
Trinity Site US Govt. Printing Office leaflet
White Sands Missile Range pamphlet 4-03w

Dept. of the Interior National Park Service information sheet
Building 1592: The von Braun Bunker, 2002 (author: Chris Ellison)
The Schleitheim Confession. (Adopted by a Swiss Brethren Conference, February 24, 1527, Brotherly Union of a Number of Children of God concerning Seven Articles)
White Sands Missile Park guide
Hiroshima Peace Memorial Ceremony programme August 6 2003

the websites:

The Manhattan Project Heritage Preservation Association Inc.
The History of the Atomic Bomb
Yucca Mountain
CommonDreams.org
The Seattle Times
The Brookings Institution
&
www.pcf.city.hiroshima.jp/virtual museum
http://www.inicom.com/hibakusha/
www.law.umkc.edu/faculty/projects/ftrials/salem/SALEM.htm
www.operationpaperclip.info/
www.denix.osd.mil/denix/Public/ES-Programs/Conservation /Legacy/ Combine/wsmrdoc.I.html
www.state.nv.us/nucwaste/yucca/seismo
http://wcatwc.ark.noaa.gov/message000588-01.htm
www.killinghope.org

the sayings & writings of

J Robert Oppenheimer (1904–1967), theoretical physicist, University of California at Berkeley, Scientific Director of the Manhattan Project

the prophecies of

Joseph Smith (1805–1844), Prophet of the Church of Jesus Christ of Latter Day Saints

fragments from the songs:

Little Red Rooster; Mr Highway Man; from *Cadillac Daddy*, Memphis 1952 (recorded by Howlin' Wolf)

'Jesus Hits Like an Atom Bomb'; Lowell Blanchard and the Valley Trio (1950)
'Guantanamera'; lyrics by Jose Fernández Díaz; 1st verse from poem by José Martí 'Yo soy un hombre sincero' in *Versos sencillos*
'Reincarnated Souls'; 1976 Bunny Wailer
'All Things Must Pass'; 1970 George Harrison
'Mercury Blues'; 1960 KC Douglas
'Beer for My Horses'; 2003 Toby Keith & Willie Nelson
'Chain Gang Blues'; 1925 Ma Rainey
'Canción del Mariachi'; 1998 Los Lobos
'No Particular Place To Go'; 1964 Chuck Berry
'Mariposa Traicionera'; 2002 Maná (from *Revolución de Amor*)
'San Francisco (Be Sure To Wear Some Flowers In Your Hair)'; 1967 Scott McKenzie
'Jin Jin / Firefly'; 1999 Takashi Hirayasu & Bob Brozman
'Natty Dread'; 1975 Bob Marley
'Atomic Love'; 1953 Caesar Little and the Red Callender Sextette

singers of songs for which I can't find fuller details

Ray Charles 1961
Bob Dylan
George Baker 1975
Roy Rogers 1930s
Louis Armstrong song 1931
Nat King Cole 1946; lyrics Bobby Troup

& traditional & anonymous songs

'Home on the Range'; trad. cowboy song
'La Cucaracha'; trad. Mexican song
trad. song of Kushida
trad. Spirituals

governmental statements, bulletins etc.

US Federal Register May 19 2003 (vol 68 no 96)
US Dept of the Interior Bureau of Land Management leaflet BLM/BM/Gi-01/015+9212
US Code: Title 36.129 National Pearl Harbor Remembrance Day
US House of Representatives debate on Administration's Nuclear Weapons Initiatives May 20 2004
Nevada Site Office USDOE National Nuclear Security Administration Yucca Mountain Project Office statement June 14 2002

US Nuclear Energy Fact (sic) Sheet
War Dept. Release on New Mexico atomic bomb test July 16 1945
US Govt. Printing Office booklet 2000-844-916 (printed on recycled paper)
Japanese Ministry of Justice Penal Code 1907

as well as:

the Mormon Battalion list of Privates enlisted to fight in Mexican-American War / la intervención norteamericana

& informational labels:

Hiroshima National Peace Memorial Hall for the Atomic Bomb Victims

from the poetry of :
Basho Matsuo (death poem)
Robert Burns ('Comin' Thro the Rye')

& in addition:

US Disembarkation Form (air flight issue to non-US Nationals)
Car stickers
Road signs (inc. Highway & 'Historic')
Graffiti
Farm signs
Shop & library signs
Fortune cookies
Hoardings
Map legends
Missile names (& synonyms from Norse mythology)
Names of the original inhabitants of the SW US deserts

www.ingramcontent.com/pod-product-compliance
Lightning Source LLC
Chambersburg PA
CBHW021327190426
43193CB00039B/417